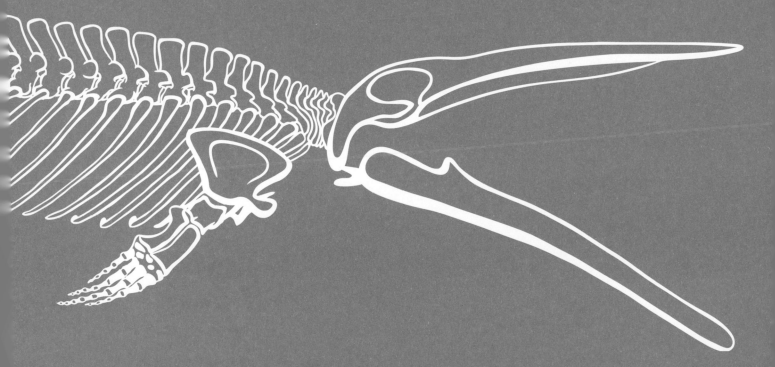

BIG BLUE FOREVER

The Story
of Canada's
Largest
Blue Whale
Skeleton

ANITA MIETTUNEN

Red Deer Press

Published in Canada by Red Deer Press, 195 Allstate Parkway, Markham, Ontario L3R 4T8

Published in the United States by Red Deer Press, 311 Washington Street, Brighton, Massachusetts 02135

All inquiries should be addressed to Red Deer Press, 195 Allstate Parkway, Markham, Ontario L3R 4T8.

www.reddeerpress.com

10 9 8 7 6 5 4 3 2

Red Deer Press acknowledges with thanks the Canada Council for the Arts, and the Ontario Arts Council for their support of our publishing program. We acknowledge the financial support of the Government of Canada through the Canada Book Fund (CBF) for our publishing activities.

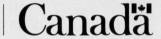

Library and Archives Canada Cataloguing in Publication
Miettunen, Anita, author
   Big blue forever : the story of Canada's largest blue whale skeleton
/ Anita Miettunen.

Includes bibliographical references and index.
ISBN 978-0-88995-542-4 (hardback)

   1. Baleen whales–Collection and preservation–Juvenile literature.
2. Marine mammal remains (Archaeology)–Exhibitions–Juvenile literature.
3. Baleen whales–Juvenile literature. 4. Beaty Biodiversity Museum–
Exhibitions–Juvenile literature. I. Title.

QL737.C42M54 2017   j599.5074'71133   C2017-903475-5

Publisher Cataloging-in-Publication Data (U.S)
Names: Miettunen, Anita, author.
Title: Big Blue forever / Anita Miettunen.
Description: Markham, Ontario : Red Deer Press, 2017. | Includes bibliographic references
   and index. | Summary: "*Big Blue Forever* is the story of the blue whale skeleton on permanent
   display at the Beaty Biodiversity Museum. The story is complemented with facts about blue
   whales and their environment, and the process museums go through to uncover, prepare and
   reassemble skeletons for display and study" – Provided by publisher.
Identifiers: ISBN 978-0-88995-542-4 (hardcover)
Subjects: LCSH: Blue whale – Juvenile literature. | Whales – Juvenile literature. | Museum
   exhibits – Juvenile literature. | BISAC: JUVENILE NONFICTION / Science & Nature /
   Environmental Conservation & Protection.
Classification: LCC QL737.C424M548 | DDC 599.5248 – dc23

Edited for the Press by Peter Carver
Cover and interior design by Kong Njo
Cover image and endpaper art: Derek Tan – Beaty Biodiversity Museum
Printed by Regent, Hong Kong.

In memory of Markku,
a wonderful brother who was at home by the ocean.
And for my children, Sonja and Margot.

– A. M.

On a windswept shoreline of Prince Edward Island something has washed ashore. It is big. It is very big. It is a great big whale. But she lives no more.

Word spreads across the island and people gather to look.
"It is as big as a boat!" a boy says.
   "At least as long as two buses," a woman says.
   A young child walks all around the whale. "She is so huge."
   "She is a blue whale," a man says.

"**H**ow did she die?" somebody asks.

"Did she get sick?"

"Was it pollution?"

"She might have been struck by a ship," a woman says.

Officials arrive and look over the whale.

"She can't stay here," one of them says, "she'll rot and smell."

"How will you get rid of her?" someone asks.

The officials wander back and forth along the beach.

"How did she die?" somebody asks.

"Did she get sick?"

"Was it pollution?"

"She might have been struck by a ship," a woman says.

Officials arrive and look over the whale.

"She can't stay here," one of them says, "she'll rot and smell."

"How will you get rid of her?" someone asks.

The officials wander back and forth along the beach.

"She'll need to be moved," one of them finally says. "We're going to bury her."

"But why?" someone asks.

"A blue whale is rare," the official says. "We think if we bury her, then over time, only her bones will remain. Perhaps one day, her skeleton will be of use to science. Or even to a museum where people can learn about her."

And so the whale is buried. She lies peacefully in the red clay soil for many years.

Then, one winter day, a scientist and his team arrive all the way from British Columbia. They have a map. And a special plan. They want to find the blue whale and dig up her skeleton.

"She hasn't been seen for twenty years!" someone says.

"Where could she be?" they wonder.

At last, they find a bone. But when they dig deeper, there is a surprise. The island soil has preserved the whole whale. Her skin is still blue! And there is a terrible smell! But the scientists are excited that they have found the whale. They will return in the spring to dig her all up.

In late spring, a field team arrives. The great dig begins to unearth the whale. The first whiff of the rotting flesh is like an explosion. The stench blasts everywhere and chases away curious onlookers. It sticks on everything and it's smothering and it's hard to breathe. But in the stinky pit, the scientists do not give up.

It is hard work to remove the flesh and blubber from the bones. One by one, each bone is collected. A blue whale's skeleton has so many pieces! The scientists want to find each one so that they can rebuild her skeleton. They want people to see the skeleton of the largest animal that ever lived.

Every bone is cleaned. Every bone is counted. Every bone is labeled.

But wait a minute, there are missing bones! The whole left flipper is gone! The scientists are stunned. How can they rebuild a skeleton if a giant piece is missing? Then they discover chain saw marks.

"Maybe when the whale washed ashore, somebody sawed off the flipper," someone guesses. "For a souvenir."

"Let's ask around the island for clues," another says.

The next day, the missing flipper bones are found! A man returns some of them to the lead scientist. Together they unearth more bones in the nearby woods.

"Thank goodness," the lead scientist says. "Now we can continue with our plan!"

Finally, everything is ready. All the bones are carefully packed into a huge truck. The whale's going to leave Prince Edward Island and start out on a cross-Canada road trip! To British Columbia.

After the long journey, the truck arrives at a workshop. Everyone is excited. Most people there have never seen a blue whale before. Most people have never worked on anything so big. They are awed by the size of her bones.

"Some of these bones are so large," a man says, "we'll need three people to move each one."

"And a cart to wheel them around," another says. A giant crane lifts the biggest bones of all.

The scientists have another problem. The stench of the dead whale lingers. The bones are filled with rancid oil that must be removed. But no one is sure how to do this.

The scientists try some experiments. They soak a few bones in a special enzyme bath with bacteria to digest the oil. They heat up the massive tanks.

"Oh, no! The bones are disintegrating!" someone says.

"We'll never build a whale skeleton if the bones turn to mush," another says.

"But we can't build a skeleton with smelly bones either!"

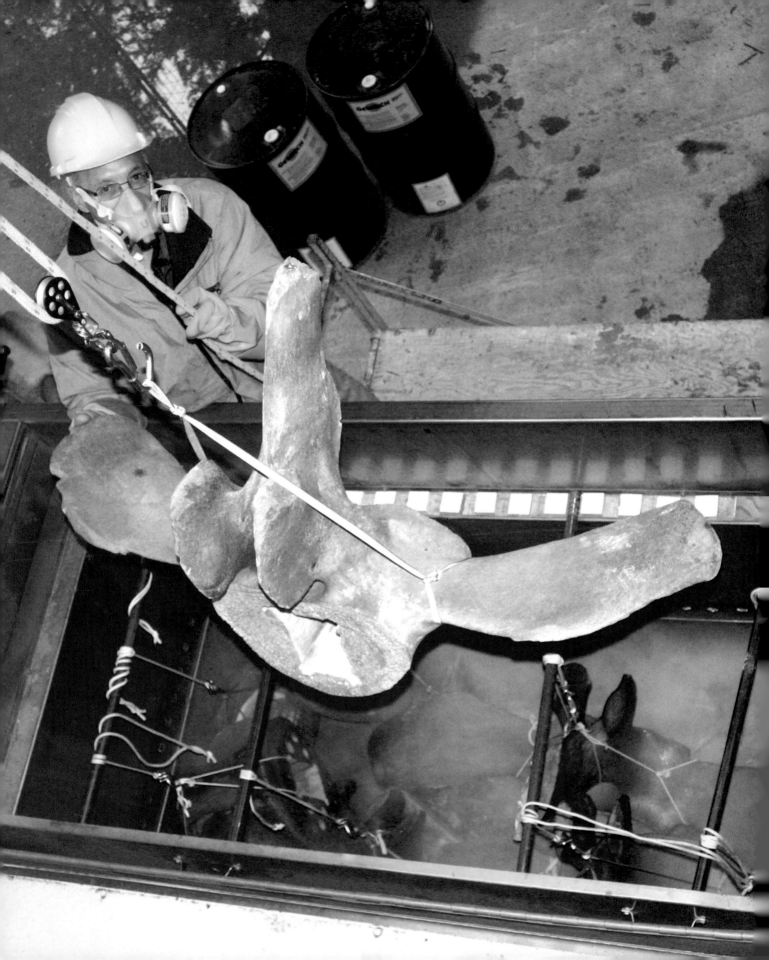

The scientists have a new idea. They set up a giant vapour degreaser machine. They add a few bones and wait and wait until . . .

The hot vapour spurts out the oil. The foul odour is gone!

By now many of the bones are badly cracked and some are broken. So painters, sculptors, and artists arrive to repair them. The workshop is abuzz. Groups of school children come to watch the scientists and artists working on the enormous skeleton.

"When it's rebuilt," a woman says, "she'll float high in a museum for everyone to see."

The bones are ready. The scientists lay out the pieces and slowly put them back together again.

"It's like a giant jigsaw puzzle!" someone says. Each piece must fit just right to rebuild the whale's skeleton. Sometimes, it seems like there are too many pieces. But then . . .

One by one, the bones connect. Flippers and a ribcage begin to form.

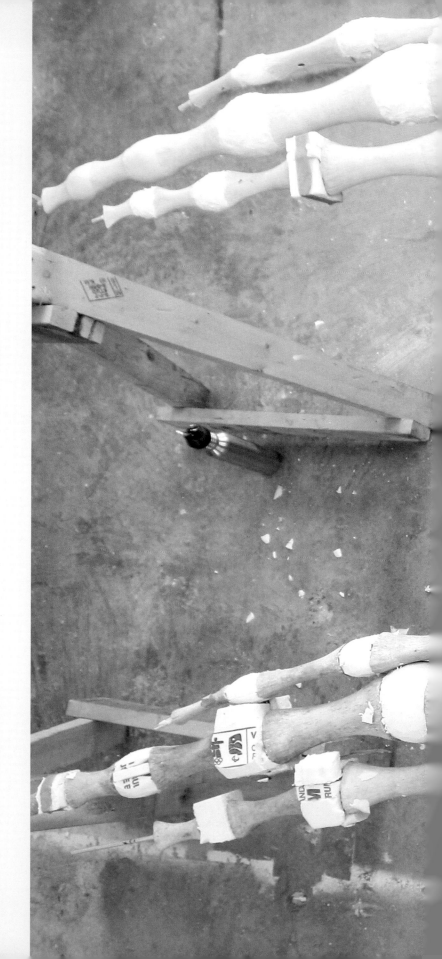

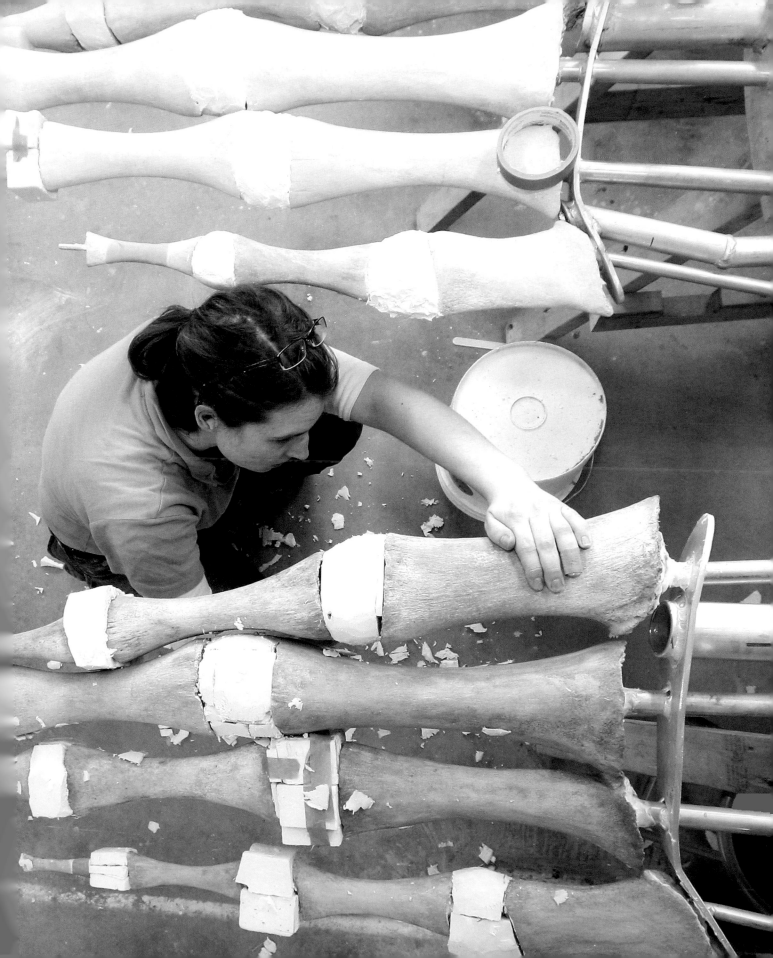

The scientists can only assemble parts of the skeleton.
The whale is too big for the workshop.
   "We'll have to put everything together at the museum,"
a man says. So they load the sections into a truck bound
for their new home.

At last, everyone's hard work pays off. The whale's skeleton is whole again. People arrive at the museum and wonder at the whale, which soars above them.

"How many bones does it have?" a boy asks.

"Almost two hundred," a woman says. "That's fewer than you have, but each bone is much bigger."

"She's larger than any dinosaur that ever lived," someone says.

A young child stretches beneath her. "She is so big."

"She is a blue whale," a scientist says. "We call her Big Blue. A long time ago, she was struck by a ship and died. But now, her story can be shared with everyone."

This book is the true story of Big Blue,
the world's largest skeleton exhibit suspended
without external armature.
At 85 feet (26 metres) long, it is the largest
blue whale skeleton exhibited in Canada,
and one of only twenty-one worldwide.
She was buried near the shore of Prince Edward
Island on the east coast of Canada for
over twenty years. In 2008, she was excavated
and moved over 6,000 kilometres to the
west coast of Canada. Big Blue's skeleton is on
permanent display at the Beaty Biodiversity
Museum at the University of
British Columbia in Vancouver, BC.

How Did Big Blue Die?

All large whales are at risk from being hit by ships. Scientists believe Big Blue was killed by a ship strike. When they examined her, they found damage to her skull, which suggested she may have died from a collision with a ship. There was no evidence of any other cause, such as entanglement in fishing gear, to explain her death. It is not likely she died of natural causes.

The Story of Big Blue

In 1987, Big Blue died and washed ashore on a remote beach at Nail Pond, near Tignish, Prince Edward Island (PEI). Personnel from the College of the Atlantic in Bar Harbor, Maine in the United States came to take some samples and they identified the blue whale as a mature female. Officials from the PEI government and Ottawa's Canadian Museum of Nature decided to bury her. They hoped that, over time, the whale would naturally decay in the ground, and eventually, if only her skeleton remained, it might be dug up one day for scientific research or public display in a museum. So machines arrived to drag the massive whale off the beach and excavate her burial hole.

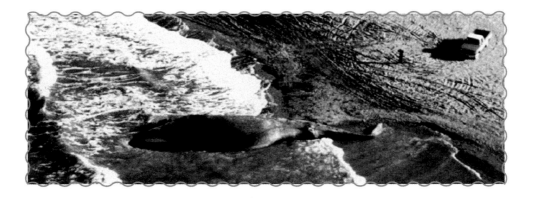

Big Blue was buried for over twenty years and few people knew about her. It was only in 2007, when Dr. Andrew Trites, a marine mammal specialist at the University of British Columbia (UBC), began searching for a large skeleton for a museum display, that he discovered there was a blue whale buried in PEI. A blue whale skeleton was exactly what he had in mind for the new Beaty Biodiversity Museum, which was being built at UBC.

After arrangements were made between UBC, the PEI government, and the Canadian Museum of Nature, it was agreed the whale skeleton could be recovered and find a new home at the Beaty Biodiversity Museum. But first, the lead scientist, Dr. Trites, needed to confirm the condition of the whale's bones after they'd been buried for more than twenty years. So, in December 2007, a small team from British Columbia (BC), led by Dr. Trites, travelled across the country to PEI in search of the blue whale.

In PEI, the team met up with Dr. Pierre-Yves Daoust, from the Atlantic Veterinary College at the University of Prince Edward Island, along with his colleagues, Dr. Scott McBurney and Dr. María Forzán, and several veterinary students. A veterinarian and specialist in wildlife pathology, Dr. Daoust was to lead the field forensics when it came time to dig up the whale. The team began searching for the

blue whale with a hand-drawn map where, long ago, a PEI conservation officer had marked the whale's grave.

As an excavator began moving the soil, a bone was located—they had found the whale! But, as the dig continued, the scientists were amazed to discover that most of the whale still had all of its flesh, blubber, and blue-tinged skin. They spent hours with shovels and hand tools, digging and prying away at the whale's tissue, to remove some bones. They wanted to make sure the bones were still in good enough condition to be used in a skeleton display.

1) The buried blue whale had hardly decayed in the red soil.

2) The team had to dig by hand to reach the whale's skeleton.

3) The veterinary team checked over the whale's vertebrae.

Once the team knew that the whale bones were suitable, they covered up the whale again and made plans to return the next spring with a larger team to dig up the whole whale.

In May 2008, the recovery of the skeleton began. An excavator dug around the whale and the team used shovels, pickaxes, crowbars, and knives to slowly remove the whale's flesh, blubber, and skin. But the tough tissue quickly dulled the knives. Keeping them sharpened was a full-time job. Finding, cleaning, and labeling all of the bones was painstaking work. And all the while, it was impossible to escape from the terrible odour wafting from the rancid oil in the bones. Finally, after ten days, the team finished excavating and preparing the bones. They loaded the bones into a truck, bound for a warehouse thousands of kilometres away, in Victoria, BC. There, scientists planned to remove the smelly oil in the bones and then reconstruct the skeleton for museum display.

The Missing Flipper

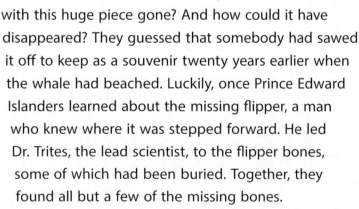

When the scientists unearthed the blue whale, they discovered there was no left flipper. A blue whale's flipper is more than 10 feet long (3 metres), with over 30 bones. How could they rebuild the skeleton with this huge piece gone? And how could it have disappeared? They guessed that somebody had sawed it off to keep as a souvenir twenty years earlier when the whale had beached. Luckily, once Prince Edward Islanders learned about the missing flipper, a man who knew where it was stepped forward. He led Dr. Trites, the lead scientist, to the flipper bones, some of which had been buried. Together, they found all but a few of the missing bones.

1) It took days in the smelly pit to recover every bone.

2) The giant skull was cut in half to help transport and clean it.

3) The bones were pressure washed to remove all the flesh.

1

2 3

Once the bones were oil-free, from January to April 2010, they were put back together to complete the skeleton. During this process, known as the articulation phase, sculptors, painters, and artists repaired many of the bones that were cracked and broken. A few pieces were so badly damaged that experts with experience in recasting dinosaur bones also helped.

How to Clean a Skeleton

A whale's bones are porous and filled with a lot of oil. How did the scientists manage to clean out the oil from inside Big Blue's bones? First, the project team built special degreasing tanks that could fit the bones. Next, they sprayed the bones with an enzyme to help break down the oil that was bonded to the bones. Then they soaked the bones for many months in a special bath with bacteria that could digest the oil. This degreasing phase removed much of the oil. But it was taking too long. The scientists needed to get all the bones oil-free as fast as possible so that the skeleton would be ready for the museum's grand opening. A few scientists tried increasing the temperature of the bath. This speeded up the

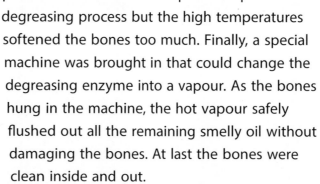

degreasing process but the high temperatures softened the bones too much. Finally, a special machine was brought in that could change the degreasing enzyme into a vapour. As the bones hung in the machine, the hot vapour safely flushed out all the remaining smelly oil without damaging the bones. At last the bones were clean inside and out.

1) The bones soaked for many months in a special degreasing bath.

2) Artists helped prepare the cleaned bones for final display.

3) The whale's jawbone was split for cleaning and then repaired.

In April 2010, Big Blue was delivered to the Beaty Biodiversity Museum in Vancouver, BC. It took another month for all of her bone sections to be pieced together and installed in the museum. Finally, after two years of dedicated teamwork since the whale's recovery in PEI, Big Blue's skeleton was ready. In a special ceremony on May 22, 2010, Big Blue's completed skeleton was unveiled for the first time.

How to Dust a Skeleton

Big Blue was installed at the Beaty Biodiversity Museum in May 2010. After five years on display, she needed to be dusted. But it isn't easy to dust a huge skeleton that is hanging high in the air. In November 2015, Mike deRoos and Michi Main arrived at the museum. Using a special lift, they were able to get close up to Big Blue and use a vacuum to dust her off. Big Blue also got a complete check up. Mike and Michi wanted to make sure her bones were not cracking or needing repairs. They were happy to find that Big Blue's bones were in great shape.

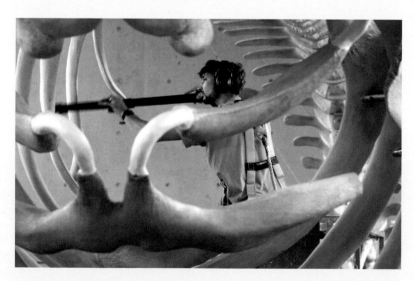

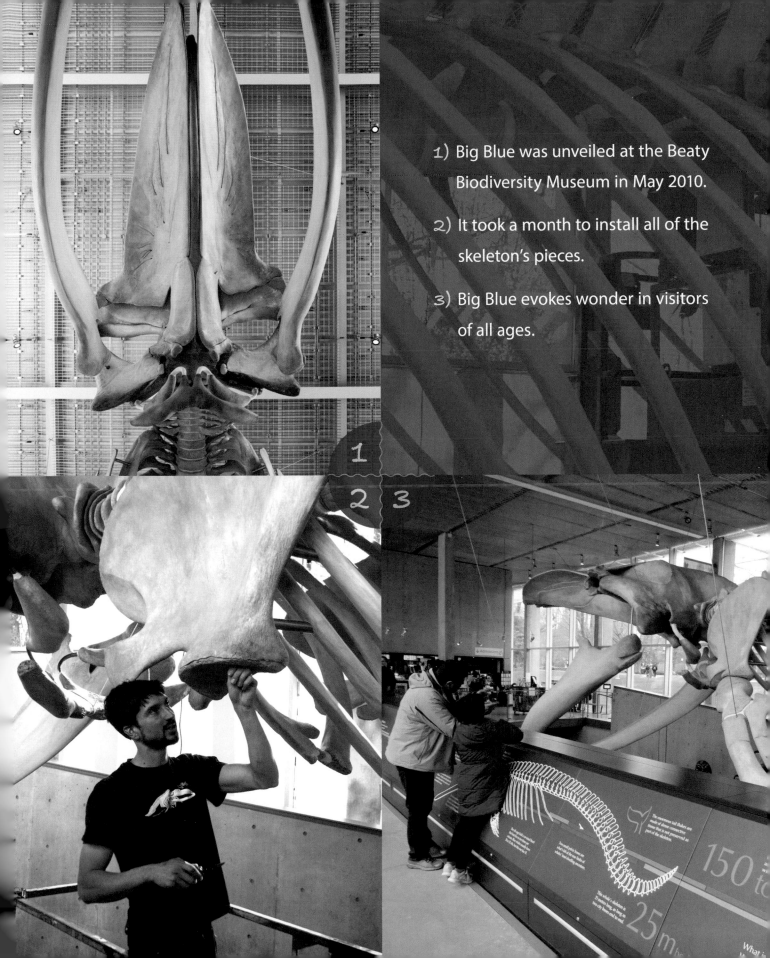

1) Big Blue was unveiled at the Beaty Biodiversity Museum in May 2010.

2) It took a month to install all of the skeleton's pieces.

3) Big Blue evokes wonder in visitors of all ages.

1
2 3

What Happens When a Whale Dies?

When a giant whale dies a natural death, it falls a long way down to the bottom of the ocean, a journey that can be more than four kilometres. It will sink quickly, as its lungs collapse. And because it drops down quickly, scavengers don't have time to feed on it. The whale's body reaches the deep ocean floor in one piece. But once there, remarkable things happen.

A whole new life cycle begins.

There are not a lot of energy sources on the ocean bottom. So a dead whale's body attracts scavenger species looking for a meal. The whale's tissues and oil-filled bones are energy rich. They become food for many other species including micro-organisms such as bacteria, and sharks, hagfish, crabs, snails, and worms. They even create a habitat for species that move in and live right on the carcass.

Over time, as bacteria, and other species feed on the carcass, the whale decays. Only the bones remain. Then new species arrive to feed, attracted by the oil in the bones and the chemicals generated by bacteria. Eventually, some species live right on the bones.

Scientists are making many new and exciting discoveries about whale falls. They have even found, at the bottom of the ocean, over thirty different kinds of bone-eating worms.

Of course Big Blue did not die a natural death. But when she died and was buried in Prince Edward Island, people thought that over time her body would naturally decay. They thought that the bacteria in the soil would digest her tissues and only her bones would be left. But the clay-like soil did not have enough oxygen or the right kind of bacteria for this to happen. Even after being buried for over twenty years, Big Blue's body was preserved—right down to her bluish skin.

About the Team

There were many people who helped make the blue whale project a success. What inspired some of the key team members to work on this unique project?

DR. ANDREW TRITES – *Lead Scientist*

"Seeing the looks of children and overhearing bits of their conversations with their parents and friends as they stand in awe next to the blue whale skeleton gives me incredible satisfaction and hope for the future. Big Blue is an inspiration to everyone who sees and hears about her. She is bigger than life with a legacy that will outlive us all as she patiently educates people about the urgent need to conserve and protect all species we share our planet with—from the smallest to the biggest."

Dr. Andrew Trites led the blue whale project. He is a Professor and Director of the Marine Mammal Research Unit in the Institute for the Oceans and Fisheries at the University of British Columbia. Dr. Trites has studied marine mammals in the North Pacific for over 30 years. His research interests include marine mammal conservation and finding ways to resolve conflicts between people and marine mammals.

MIKE DEROOS – *Skeleton Articulator*

"I feel as though nature is increasingly overlooked in our busy world; my hope is that the bones and story of this amazing whale will inspire a curiosity and respect for all life on this planet for generations to come."

Mike deRoos is a master skeleton articulator, biologist, and builder, who designed Big Blue's magnificent lunge-feeding skeleton display. He is an expert in articulating marine mammal skeletons, right from recovering carcasses, to designing and installing anatomically correct skeleton displays.

MICHI MAIN – *Project Manager and Assistant Articulator*

"It's about connection for me. While we creatively overcome new challenges in each project and puzzle the pieces of our skeletons together, we connect ourselves intimately with the natural world and with each other."

Michi Main studied marine ecology and conservation biology in university. As project manager and assistant articulator on the blue whale project, she oversaw the collection, labeling, and organization of the hundreds of pieces of Big Blue's bones and bone fragments recovered in PEI.

DR. PIERRE-YVES DAOUST – *Field Forensics Expert*

"I am passionate about wild animals, which I have admired ever since I was young. My work allows me to learn about aspects of wild animals' lives that few people are aware of. By identifying common causes of death in wild animals, we can help prevent these deaths, particularly when they are associated with human activities. And the more we can learn about different species, the better we can appreciate and care for our world."

Dr. Pierre-Yves Daoust is a veterinarian and wildlife pathology specialist at the Atlantic Veterinary College in Prince Edward Island. He is an expert in performing autopsies in many different marine species, including mammals, birds, and sea turtles.

PROJECT TEAM

PEI VET TEAM

Essential Blue Whale Facts

Common name: **Blue whale**

Scientific name: *Balaenoptera musculus*

Blue whales are mammals. They are the biggest animals that have ever lived on earth. One blue whale can be longer than two city buses. That's even longer than a dinosaur. A blue whale's heart is the size of a small car and its arteries are big enough for a baby to crawl through.

When it's born, a blue whale calf is about the size of two minivans. In the first six months of life, it will drink a lot of its mother's milk every day—as much as 50 gallons (almost 200 litres) worth. When fully grown at six to ten years of age, a blue whale can eat over four tonnes of krill (tiny, shrimp-like creatures) every day. That's as much as the weight of an elephant!

Blue whales can live as long as seventy to eighty years. And they can weigh as much as thirty-three elephants. The blue whale at the Beaty Biodiversity Museum may have weighed 150 tonnes.

There are about 180 bones in a blue whale's skeleton. The blue whale's jawbone is the longest bone of any living animal. A jaw-dropping fact: It can measure over seven meters (twenty-two feet) in length. A living whale's bones are filled with lots of oil to help it float. About half the weight of the bones is the weight of the oil.

Blue whales live in all oceans around the world and are usually found alone or in pairs. Every year, for four to six months, they spend time feeding in nutrient-rich colder waters, where they build up their body fat, before migrating in small herds to warmer waters to calve.

Species at Risk

A species at risk is a plant or animal that is in danger of disappearing from the wild. In Canada, the Committee on the Status of Endangered Wildlife in Canada reviews "at risk" species and classifies them according to their levels of risk:

Extinct – a wildlife species that no longer exists.

Extirpated – a wildlife species that no longer exists in the wild in Canada, but exists elsewhere.

Endangered – a wildlife species facing imminent extirpation or extinction.

Threatened – a wildlife species that is likely to become endangered if nothing is done to reverse the factors leading to its extirpation or extinction.

Special Concern – a wildlife species that may become threatened or endangered because of a combination of biological characteristics and identified threats.

Data Deficient – a category that applies when there is not enough available information to determine the level of risk for a wildlife species.

Not at Risk – a wildlife species that is currently not at risk of extinction.

Source: http://www.cosewic.gc.ca/eng/sct2/sct2_6_e.cfm

An Endangered Species

Although there used to be hundreds of thousands of blue whales in the world, today, because of past commercial hunting, there are only a few thousand left. Population estimates range from 1,700 in the Southern Ocean, 600 – 1,500 in the North Atlantic, and 2,000 – 3,000 in the North Pacific. In Canada, they inhabit both coastal and open ocean waters in the Atlantic and Pacific regions, though it's rare to see them off the coast of British Columbia.

Experts estimate that there are fewer than 250 mature individuals in the Northwest Atlantic population in Canada. Whales in this population have been sighted mostly in the Gulf of St. Lawrence, off southern Newfoundland, and off the east coast of Nova Scotia. The number of blue whales off the coast of western Canada is unknown. A survey in 2007 counted five blue whales off the coast of Haida Gwaii in British Columbia. This was the most recorded for this area in the past fifty years. In August 2015, a Department of Fisheries and Oceans survey sighted two blue whales 60 nautical miles off the west coast of Vancouver Island.

In 1966, the International Whaling Commission banned the commercial hunting of blue whales. This international protection has helped to slowly increase blue whale populations, even though a few countries still continued whaling practices after 1966. The blue whale is protected in Canada but classified as endangered under the federal *Species at Risk Act*. The International Union for Conservation of Nature (IUCN) also lists the blue whale as an endangered species.

THREATS TO THE BLUE WHALE

Around the world, hunting bans and scientific research are helping to save blue whales. The result is that their numbers are slowly growing again. However, the blue whale is a species at risk and it is endangered. In Canada, there are still many threats that could affect the survival of blue whale populations. Threats to the Pacific population of blue whales off the coast of British Columbia are not well understood. Some scientists think that for the Northwest Atlantic population, because there are so few blue whales, activities that affect even a few individuals can be a problem for the species' survival.

Some of the threats to the blue whale include:

NOISE POLLUTION

Over the past fifty years, the oceans have become noisier. And scientists think this could be a high-risk threat to blue whales. Blue whales produce low frequency sounds (less than 200 Hz), although it is not known exactly why. It could be for communicating with other whales, including possible mates that are swimming nearby or far away. It could also be for exploring the environment and searching for feeding grounds, or for other behavioural reasons.

But scientists worry that the increasing ocean noise caused by human activities such as underwater seismic testing, shipping traffic, explosions, and industrial and military activities could be making it hard for whales to hear their own sounds. And these human-made noises could also be changing whale behaviour and causing them to avoid noisy areas or to pause in their normal activities such as resting, feeding, vocalizing, diving, or nurturing calves. Although these possible effects are not fully known, scientists are concerned that noise pollution may be affecting the recovery of blue whale populations. They are continuing to research this important topic to better understand how this threat can be minimized.

REDUCED FOOD SUPPLIES

Blue whales have a special diet: they mainly eat krill and they eat tonnes of it. If the amount or location of krill supplies is reduced, then this could be a high-risk threat to blue whale populations, especially if female whales don't have enough nutrition to continue with their pregnancy or to provide milk for their calves. Harvesting krill commercially is one factor that could reduce krill supplies for blue whales. However, in Eastern Canada, this activity has not been allowed since 1998. There is also concern that climate change due to human activities could affect the amount of krill in the blue whale's usual feeding grounds. But our current knowledge is not enough to predict how.

COLLISIONS WITH SHIPS

Because blue whales are so rare, we still know very little about them. Scientists who research the issue of ship strikes in Canada mostly focus on right whales. Scientists know that any ship going fast

enough could kill a whale. Depending on the size of the vessel, speeds of 12 to 15 knots (nautical miles per hour) could be deadly. Both small and large ships, ranging from 45 to over 900 feet (about 14 to 274 metres) long, have killed whales. If a ship hits a whale, people on the ship may or may not detect a bump, depending on the size of the ship. People who work in the marine shipping industry are also learning more about this important issue and trying to make changes that can help reduce ship strikes against whales.

WHALE WATCHING

The increasing popularity of whale watching activities in coastal areas is also a threat to blue whales, especially when boats approach too closely. This can disrupt whale activities such as feeding, resting, diving, breathing, mating, and nurturing of calves and if repeated, can affect species survival and conservation. Whales may also change their behaviour and be forced to move to other habitats. Some scientific data collection activities can also have an impact if this work requires getting close to whales. Research, education, and certain regulations are helping to better control whale watching disturbances and reduce this threat.

ENTANGLEMENT IN FISHING GEAR

Although blue whales are huge, powerful animals, sometimes they can accidentally get caught in fishing gear. This can lead to serious injury or even death. In some regions of Canada, there are now programs set up for training fishers in how to disentangle gear and programs for reporting on marine mammal entanglements and for responding to such emergencies.

OCEAN POLLUTION

Many kinds of chemical pollutants end up in the ocean from sources such as agriculture, industrial and municipal waste, shipping, dredging, and gas and oil activities. Although it can be difficult to track these contaminants, there is evidence that some of these human-made chemicals can affect the health of whales, including how they reproduce.

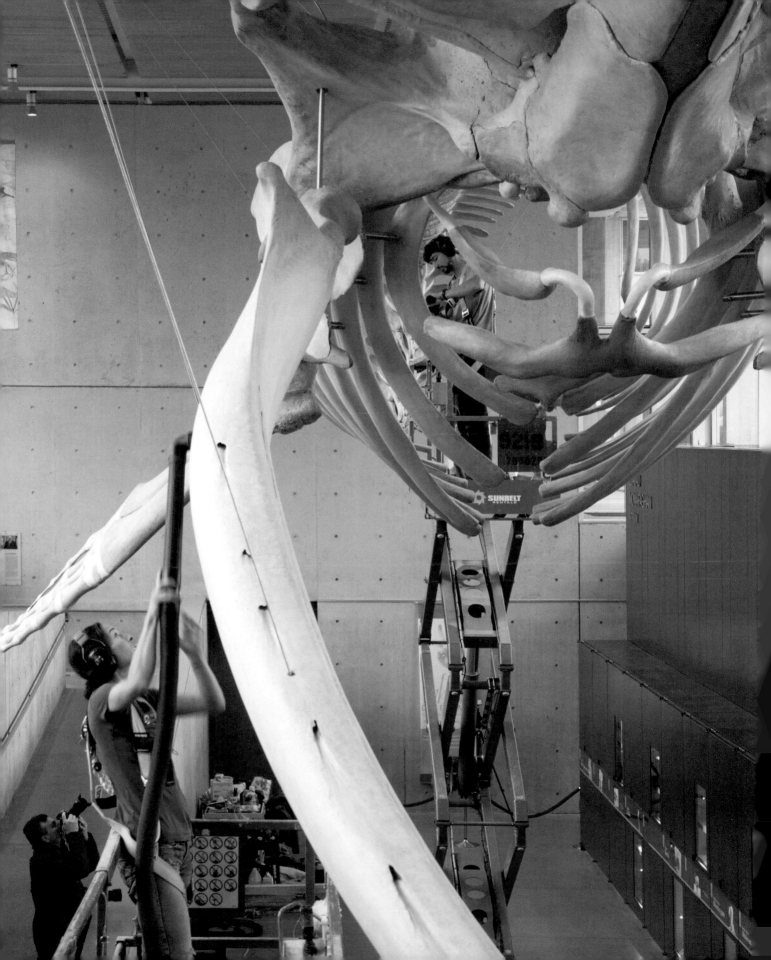

Author's Note

WHY BIG BLUE MATTERS TO US

Like many, when I first met Big Blue at the Beaty Biodiversity Museum, I was struck by the sheer size of her. Big Blue held a powerful grip on my imagination. I began to wonder about her life in the wild. How did she die? How exactly did she end up in the museum? And as a species, why was the very existence of the largest animal ever to have lived on earth now so fragile?

Although blue whales were once abundant, over-hunting caused an alarming drop in their numbers from an estimated 300,000 to just a few thousand worldwide by the early 1930s. Today, it is thought that less than 7,000 of these rare whales are left in the world. Scientific research and hunting bans are helping their numbers grow. Yet human-related activities continue to threaten blue whales.

In my research for *Big Blue Forever,* one thing became clear. Without the vision and drive of the many people involved in recovering and restoring the blue whale skeleton, many of us would be a lot poorer for not knowing about Big Blue. And hers is a story that matters. For in our busy lives, we sometimes forget about our connection to biodiversity. We may even try to ignore the impact human activities have on nature. But if we don't pay attention, we risk losing something irreplaceable. We risk losing some of the most remarkable animals that we share the planet with, like the blue whale.

It is thanks to the passionate team of scientists, and many others who dedicated their time, skills, and expertise to the blue whale project, that the public can now view Big Blue and learn more

about this endangered species. I hope young readers will enjoy
learning about Big Blue's story and about how scientists, despite
many obstacles, never gave up on their dream to reconstruct her
magnificent skeleton. I also hope my book will inspire readers
young and old to find out more about biodiversity and learn how
they can help protect earth's fragile creatures. Because once a
species is extinct, it's gone forever.

To Learn More about Blue Whales

Beaty Biodiversity Museum:
http://beatymuseum.ubc.ca/whats-on/exhibitions/permanent-exhibits/
blue-whale-display/about-blue-whales/

Blue Whale Project:
https://sites.google.com/site/bluewhaleproject/Home/fun-facts-about-
theproject

Blue Whale and Marine Mammal Skeleton Displays:
http://www.cetacea.ca/

Department of Fisheries and Oceans Canada:
http://www.dfo-mpo.gc.ca/species-especes/aquatic-aquatique/blue-whale-
rorqual-bleu-eng.htm

http://www.dfo-mpo.gc.ca/species-especes/profiles-profils/blueWhale_
Atl-rorqualbleu-eng.html

The International Union for Conservation of Nature:
http://www.iucn.org/about/work/programmes/species/

http://www.iucnredlist.org/details/2477/0

Mingan Island Cetacean Study:
http://www.rorqual.com/

Parks Canada:
http://www.pc.gc.ca/eng/nature/eep-sar/itm3/eep-sar3y/1.aspx

Acknowledgements

The blue whale project was made possible through the cooperation and efforts of many individuals and corporate sponsors:

Project leader: Andrew Trites
Master articulator: Mike deRoos
Project manager/assistant articulator: Michi Main
Assistant articulators: Bob deRoos, Jesse McBeath
Skeleton recovery team: Nicola Brabyn, Rosemary Curley, Pierre-Yves Daoust, Fiep de Bie, Jenny Ellis, María Forzán, Kendal Gallant, Mark Halpen, Darlene Jones, Sandra Keough, Bill Main, Shannon Martinson, Scott McBurney, Soraya Sayi, Chris Stinson, and Veterinary Students from the University of Prince Edward Island
Articulation team: Karen Akune, Bryce Butkiewicz, Georges Daigle, George Hudson, David Hunwick, Catherine Jacks, Alison King, Joanne Thomson, Elizabeth Thomson, Leah Thorpe, Ethan Wills
Interpretation: Natalie Bowes
Articulation advisors: Jeremy Goldbogen, Steven King, Nick Pyenson
Degreasing advisors: Doug Kilburn, Gary Lesnicki, Tony Warren
Skull casting: Gilles Danis, Frank Hadfield, Ken Kucher
Logistical support: Lebby Balakshin, Julienne Hills, Sue Kennedy, Wayne Maddison, Eve Rickert, Kim Woolcock
Graphics: Derek Tan
Media relations: Brian Lin
Structural engineering: C.C. Yao
Architectural consulting: Michael Cunningham
Volunteers: Pam Allen, Jacklyn Barrs, Morgan Davies, Brenda deRoos, Stacey Hrushowy, Ruth Joy, Aaron Keech, Sherman Lai, Ocean Lum, Bonnie Main, Meg Malone, Don McBeath, Shannon McFadyen, Brent McLean, Merina Paton, Crystal Peterson, Andrea Rambeau, Lynn Riemer, Don Walker, Mandy Wong

Corporate sponsors: Acklands Grainger Incorporated, Artworld Picture Framing and Art Supplies, British Columbia Ferry Services Incorporated (Transportation), Canadian Museum of Nature, Canadian National Railway Company (Transportation of whale PEI to Victoria), Ellice Recycle Limited (Warehouse space in Victoria), Emery E H Electric Limited, Fairey & Company Limited, McLean Foundation, Novozymes North America Incorporated (Degreasing enzymes), Nyx Dimensions (3-D scan of assembled pieces), Prince Edward Island Veterinary College, Province of Prince Edward Island, Rekord Marine Enterprises Limited, Reliance Specialty Products Incorporated, Royal Ontario Museum, Sherwood Motor Inn, UBC Bookstore (Branded merchandise), Univar Canada Limited, Van Kam Freightways Limited (Transportation of whale Victoria to UBC), Viking Air Limited, Walker's Saw Shop (Saws), Westjet Airlines Limited

---

I am grateful to several individuals, many who remain unnamed here, who supported this book project in countless ways. I especially thank Mike deRoos, Michi Main, Derek Tan, and Andrew Trites. I also thank Moira Brown and her colleagues, Pierre-Yves Daoust, Tyler DesRoches, Kelly Doyle, Darren Irwin, Mairin Kerr, Ken Kilback, Bruce MacKenzie at the *Victoria Times Colonist*, Craig Smith, and Nancy Vo. Special thanks to everyone who contributed photos; without your generosity, this book would have a lot of empty pages.

At Red Deer Press, I thank Richard Dionne and Kong Njo; and especially Peter Carver for his stellar editing and guidance.

Finally, I thank my family and friends for their invaluable support.

Image Credits

Pages 34, Alaska Fisheries Science Center, NOAA Fisheries Service; 8-9, Beaty Biodiversity Museum archives; 45, Monique Bournot-Trites; 54, John Calambokidis, Cascadia Research; 10-11, 36 top R, Bob deRoos; 22-23, Mike deRoos; 58, Ernie DesRoches; 35, DFO; 14-15, 39 bottom L and R, Jenny Ellis; 44 top R, © Yoshihiro Fujiwara/JAMSTEC courtesy of http://www.jamstec.go.jp/e/about/; 32, 43 top R and bottom L, David Gilbar; 39 top L and R, 47, Brooke Hutt; 4-5, © iStock; 46, Rosemarie Keough; 17, Bill Main; 63, Michi Main; 28-29, 43 bottom R, 48, 52, Anita Miettunen; 50-51, Mingan Island Cetacean Study (MICS); 44 top and bottom L, bottom R, Craig Smith; 18-19, 21, 40, 41 top L and R, Nick Stanger; 44 bottom, Chris Stinson; 26-27, 41 bottom L and R, Bruce Stotesbury, Victoria Times Colonist; 25, 31, 42, 43 top L, 56, 60, Derek Tan – Beaty Biodiversity Museum; 36 bottom L, 37, 38, Andrew Trites; 6-7, Shane Wilson; 13, Kim Woolcock.

Bibliography

The following sources were consulted for facts in the writing of this book:

http://beatymuseum.ubc.ca/whats-on/exhibitions/permanent-exhibits/blue-whale-display/

Beauchamp, J., Bouchard, H., de Margerie, P., Otis, N., Savaria, J.-Y., 2009. "Recovery Strategy for the blue whale (*Balaenoptera musculus*), Northwest Atlantic population, in Canada [Final]." *Species at Risk Act* Recovery Strategy Series. Fisheries and Oceans Canada, Ottawa. 62 pp. (Available here: https://www.registrelep-sararegistry.gc.ca/document/default_e.cfm?documentID=1773)

Canadian Wildlife Health Cooperative (information for reporting sick or dead wildlife): http://www.cwhc-rcsf.ca/

Department of Fisheries and Oceans. 2013. "Report on the Progress of Recovery Strategy Implementation for Blue, Fin and Sei Whales (*Balaenoptera musculus, B. physalus* and *B. borealis*) in Pacific Canadian Waters for the Period 2006-2011." *Species at Risk Act* Recovery Strategy Report Series. Fisheries and Oceans Canada, Ottawa. v + 10 pp. (Available here: http://www.registrelep-sararegistry.gc.ca/default.asp?lang=En&n=6268643B-1)

International Whaling Commission: https://iwc.int/home

Smith, C.R., A.G. Glover, T. Treude, N.D. Higgs, and D.J. Amon. 2015. "Whale-fall ecosystems: recent insights into ecology, paleoecology, and evolution." *Annual Review of Marine Science* Vol.7: 571-596. (Available here: http://www.annualreviews.org/doi/abs/10.1146/annurev-marine-010213-135144)

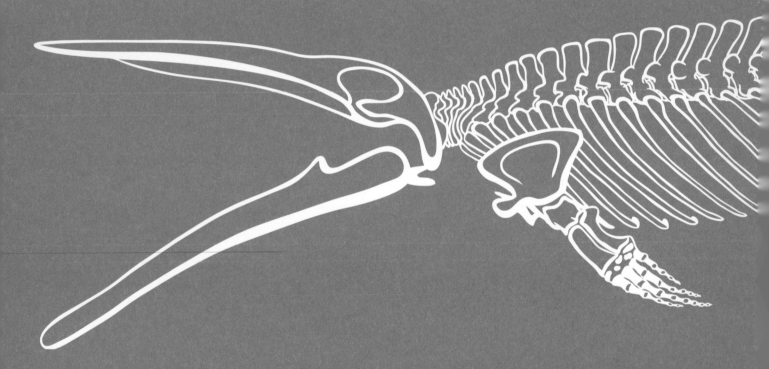